Beyond the Greenwood

HIDDEN VALLEY POETS

Published in 2024 by Hidden Valley Poets, c/o Nottinghamshire County Council
Copyright © Hidden Valley Poets

Introduction

The Hidden Valley Poets met on a poetry course run by Inspire at Ravenshead Library in early 2022. The course was part of the Miner2Major project, supported by the National Lottery Heritage Fund, celebrating the important habitats, special species and rich heritage of the Sherwood Forest area of Nottinghamshire.

You may not have heard of the Hidden Valley area of Nottinghamshire, it lies between the north of Nottingham reaching to Mansfield, stretching from Hucknall to Ollerton. The Hidden Valley is an area of contrasts - open fields, wildlife and ancient woodlands juxtaposed with remnants of industry - coal pits, disused railways and mills. We chose the name Hidden Valley for our group as we all live within this area.

After the course finished the four of us continued to meet up to write and discuss poetry. We still meet regularly to share the poems we've written and to read and be inspired by the work of other poets.

This anthology of our poetry reflects the many different facets of Nottinghamshire's Hidden Valley - its history, legends, nature, life and our times.

We hope you enjoy our poems and perhaps be inspired to find a poetry group or to write poems for yourself.

The Hidden Valley Poets are:

Anita

I've lived in Nottinghamshire since the late 1980s and love its varied history - from the industrial heritage to its myths and tales (although my heart will always remain in Derbyshire where I was born and grew up). I rediscovered my love of poetry during lockdown in 2020/21. During this time I had a Chapbook published, 'Echoes of our Lives' and took part in other Miner2Major projects with a couple of poems included in their 'Poetry Place' publication.

Being part of our poetry group is very rewarding - from writing and sharing poems to making new friends and putting this book together. I hope you enjoy reading it as much as we have writing it.

Helen

I have lived in Nottingham all my life. Previously I worked with children and families within the Newark and Sherwood area, whilst working with the Sure Start programme.

I joined the Hidden Valley Poetry Group in March 2022, after enjoying the two-week poetry course with Inspire Learning. At the time I wasn't working and found writing poetry very therapeutic. I had written poems in the past but not at this level.

I hope you find this little poetry book as inspiring as we have. Anyone can write poems - just put pen to paper and have a go. Good Luck!

Marie

After working full-time in the NHS for 30 plus years, I made the move to part-time independent practice, allowing some welcome 'me-time' ☺.

I'd dabbled with poetry in the past and took the opportunity to sign up for an Inspire poetry course. Following this I have continued developing my writing and reading of poetry as part of the Hidden Valley Poetry Group. My professional background in mental health has a big influence on my poetry, reflecting on the struggles and joys of life alongside the benefits of mindfulness and wellbeing.

Whilst being a proud Cumbrian, I have lived in this locality for over 20 years, made it my second home and have come to love the people and places of Nottinghamshire.

Wendy

Born in Bulwell, I have lived and worked in numerous parts of the county. Memories of picnics with my sister *inside* the Major Oak, retelling our version of the myths and legends of Sherwood Forest fed my interest in local traditions and history, exploring what connects people to places and to each other. Writing verse was usually just for fun – and it always rhymed! Through Inspire Learning I've discovered more about poetry as a craft I can learn, practice, and get better at (and I get to choose the subjects!).

Embarking on this journey with the Hidden Valley Poets has been a supportive and encouraging revelation and with this publication our hope is to continue the tradition of storytelling, by sharing it with you.

Acknowledgments

Thanks to Ruth Shelton who facilitated the Inspire Learning poetry course where we first met, which sparked our interest in poetry and our desire to continue learning and sharing after the course ended. Also for Ruth's suggestions and support in editing this publication.

Thanks to Miner2Major, a Landscape Partnership Scheme supported by The National Lottery Heritage Fund, which has funded the production of Beyond the Greenwood and to Steve Little, Miner2Major Scheme Manager and Karen Bonsall from Inspire Learning for their support, encouragement and for making things happen so we were able to publish this book.

Thanks to Alexandra Ghimisi for allowing us to use her painting 'The Path' for the cover. We were surrounded by her artwork on display in Ravenshead Library and it feels fitting to have her artwork included in this collection.

Thanks also to the staff at Ravenshead library for being so welcoming and providing lovely facilities for our meetings, photocopying and for showing an interest in our group.

Finally thanks to our proof readers Caroline Prance and Mandy Martin for their valuable time and input.

Foreword

I knew I was going to enjoy this book from the off when each of the poets introduced themselves with only their first names. This is indicative of the very open and personable nature of these poems. Anita, Helen, Marie and Wendy talk to us as fellow humans and their words are accessible and inclusive.

This is the poetry of the Hidden Valley Poets and for all its variety of shape, tone and subject there is a consistency of voice with a solid sense of place, 'Beyond the Greenwood' draws upon the rich heritage of the region and reflects its accent and life with love.

This collection is a joy to read - like chatting with friends and the photos enhance the experience perfectly.

Henry Normal
Writer, Poet, Radio Presenter, TV/Film Producer

Index

Into the Greenwood

I believe
in fairytales
of ladies
and their knights
of dragons and kings
mythical things
the balance between
darkness and light.
I also believe
in tomorrows,
in things
we may never see.
It's my belief
if it's in the heart
there's every chance
it can be.

Wendy

What Feet

have trod upon these stone stairs,
smooth tracks worn into matching dips?

How did it feel beneath the soles
of leather shoes or wooden clogs?

Step Step
on   on
Step   Step

Mother, daughter, father, son;
generations come and gone.

Anita

Wellow Dancer

I want to be the May Queen,
I want to be a maypole dancer.
But living outside the village, wistfully
I watched local girls take their turn.
Weaving their colourful silk ribbons
in and out around that majestic pole,
dancing in time to the music.

I knew nothing of the meaning,
the end of the winter season.
A welcome observance of spring,
a nod to nature and celebration
of fertility and the feminine.
I just wanted to dance and hold those
pretty ribbons in my small hands.

Marie

Work House 1826

A mother and child.
Where are dreams when penniless and poor,
no food and shelter, nowhere to go.
Mother and child briefly together, cold and grey.
She sleeps on hard floor, with a pillow of straw,
rest does not come easy.
Sounds of jangling keys and barking coughs
stay with her,
she longs for her child and prays for survival.
Thankful he is too young to work,
hers is hard and boring,
many hours on her knees, scrubbing floors.
Idle souls punished, forced to repeat tasks.
Her child is taken! An inhuman cry
among jangling keys, barking coughs.
No rest. She dreams of Sunday.
What does she see - her child's face on the far
side of the chapel?
A glimpse of torn trousers she had tried to mend,
the red curls just like his dad.

Helen

Not from Notts?

Dunna whittle if tha canna understand wot ah sez
Int su common to 'ear these days,
All t'owd words n sayins. Keep yer tabs flappin' n
Listen 'ard, yuh might lairn summat
Enlightnin'. Dunna get a
Cob on! Thes no point chuntering yuh
Taitered. Let's ay a mash an try agen.

Translation
(for those unfamiliar with the dialect)

Don't worry if you can't understand all I say
It isn't so common to hear these days,
All the old words and sayings. Pay attention and
Listen hard, you might learn something
Enlightening. But don't get
Cross! There's no point complaining you're
Tired. Let's have a cup of tea and another go.

Anita

The Territorial Wolf

Finally arrived on holiday, lovely accommodation,
four bedrooms/two baths/private peaceful garden.
As the tea brewed, he explored upstairs
lights went on, and off and on,
cupboards and drawers squeaked open.
"Hey, come up and choose, all got great views."
His suitcase reclined, in the first room
spilling t-shirts and socks across the runner.
Next door a wardrobe revealed his posse of shirts
on hangers still swinging, jostling
along the rail.
The en-suite double was, surprisingly,
already equipped
with his toiletries and hand towel on the floor.
Fourth bedroom was in the attic.
Its TV sending morse code to a remote,
pinned under his briefcase.
"What do you think?" he said, beaming.
"It's great" I said -
"A real home from home".

Wendy

The Journey

Fred lived alone with little distraction,
he wanted some fun and satisfaction.
The weather was horrid, it started to rain,
he browsed the timetable and boarded a train.
He looked up and down to find the right seat.

A lady sat opposite he tried to engage,
disinterested, she looked down at her page.
Fred didn't give up and gave another look,
this time she blushed and looked up from her book.

His journey would end at Nottingham, 20 miles to go,
plenty of time for her affection to grow.
They left the train, hand in hand,
and together set off to see a brass band.

Helen

SHERWOOD

So much more than Robin
Hood and the majestic oak
Ey up mi duck and fuddles galore
Romance and ghosts at Annesley Hall
Wellow maypole dancing queen
Observatory skies previously unseen
Open exhibitions at Patchings Farm
Druids altar sun aligned charm

Marie

The Legend Underfoot

A black coated swarm converge at the gates
head for sanctuary under towering headstocks
hidden from the demands of life, the
expectations of heart and hearth,
they are the men of Sherwood
heading for the County Larder

While ever the lamps are burning below,
find them picking a way through the face,
burrowing, bending, bonding
chocks and props on a seamless path
taking the men of Sherwood
deep inside the County Larder

Work for independence, work long to live in
houses that will never be their own
it's a different view of freedom
from the bottom of a water logged shaft
celebrate the men of Sherwood
the last in the County Larder

Wendy

Blidworth Brass

It was a hard day's graft
in dark and dust,
surviving the perils,
awaiting the pint.

Later........ sipping, gulping,
chatting and laughing.
Breathing   being
together, family and friends.

Still, a safe warm hub,
the Christmas performance
with cornets, horns
tuba and trombones.

The Miners' Welfare Club,
generations surviving, thriving,
a home for them all.

Marie

Bread or Blood!

In Arnold we massed,
first to gather around Ned Ludd,
smashing machines that steal our livelihood,
letting owd Enoch do our work
as we chant 'Bread or blood! Bread or blood!'

Powered looms enslave us,
take skills from our hands,
starve us in a steam-driven land.
Unions banned, our voices ignored,
profit is the only lord.

John Booth with his final breath
called out for a minister. He begged,
'can you keep a secret?'
Yes, came back the fervent lie,
'Aye lad, so can I'.

Our brotherhood is strong,
shoulder to shoulder
together we stand.
They send soldiers to take us,
write laws to break us.

Death
the price for machine breakers.

Anita

Clippo

A place in time,
standing cold and empty.
A shadow of former glory,
nature has taken over.
An empty shell,
traditions lost,
memories gone.
Once man and boy accepted their fate,
taking snap box, hat and lamp.
Greeting each other with
ey up me duck.
Blackened with dust,
fresh air finally reached.
Pint in the local,
soak in tin bath.
Factory fortnight,
pit shut down for two weeks.
Ponies see light of day.
Time to rest.

Helen

Disappeared

I remember the miners toiling in pits
from Calverton, Linby, Gedling
to Newstead, Bestwood, Blidworth.
Descending
daily into dark and danger.
Dust
that lingered on skin, in lungs,
as they crawled
       to reach black gold.

The coal lorry depositing
rumbling shards of sound.
Nuggets tumbled and rolled
into hessian sacks
hoisted swiftly onto backs
bent
under their weight.
Racing up paths to tip each load
into every coal bunker for every home.
Warmth,
       for cold winter days.

I remember the housewives
after delivery done
with dustpan and brush,
kneeling
on roads. Every spill swept,
every bit kept.
Eeking it out, make do and mend,
cleaning the grate, donkey stoned steps.
Standards
        to maintain.

Disappeared in time,
in mines closed,
smokeless zones.
In central heating
and modern homes.

Anita

Skylark

I rise, I rise
climb and climb,
high
on the notes of my tune,
exulting into the sky.

Weaving a lace of joy,
open my heart
in breathless song
above green fields
receding into patchwork.

Hear my tune!
I sing
to mark my home,
all that I hold dear
below and above.

Anita

Life After Life

Rain crashes from oak to elder to fern
alights on the ground and trembles
she keeps to a manicured edge
her footsteps hidden beneath diamonds
a sense of belonging
450 years of knowing
and still the doors are locked.
Rosemary and thyme offer solace as
she passes into the arms of
a rolling mist of memories that
pull her down the hill, to the gate
where men gather, dogs bark.
Soon they'll find the mermaid trap.
Soon she'll have to go back.

Wendy

Sunrise

Looking out the window,
a garden full of life,
Chaffinch, squirrels,
scurrying   in flight.

Standing on the step,
I see bulbs peeping, buds tight,
making an appearance,
searching   for light.

Stepping out the door,
walking round the block,
my head clears, my thoughts
begin   to unlock.

Step by step, I take comfort,
from the wonder all around,
knowing tomorrow,
sunrise   will be found.

Marie

The Robin

I never tire of looking for you,
you are so brave and true.
Cares in your world are few,
if only I could be like you.

It must feel wonderful
to fly and fly wherever you will.
To be so light, with little care,
If only I could be like you.

Your song lifts my spirit,
I love to hear you sing.
Your needs so small it's true,
If only I could be like you.

Helen

21

All Weathers

Love is a changeable climate
hot and shivery
magical snow
thunder and lightning
all aglow.

Stormy and silent
arid and cold
foggy and uncertain
you need the right clothes

for the riskiest weather
moderate, indifferent
and dull.

Marie

Change

The winds of change so often are scary.
No wonder many are wary.
For some change is a breeze,
for others it is anything but ease.
Hold tight and enjoy the ride.

Helen

Round Our Way

Alternative
spaces
reshape the
community

Rhythms
echo
blameless
immunity

Realistic
timescales
enable
opportunity

Worlds
besides worlds
safe from
obscurity

Wendy

25

Papplewick Church

Standing firm for nine centuries,
a constant in our lives.
Many prayed in your house,
seeking solace and peace.
You have witnessed it all,
war, death, grief, birth and new love.
Your bells ringing with comfort and joy.
In your garden is a bench.
A place of stillness,
a picture of calm.
Sweet smelling flowers,
beautiful bird song.
Allen a Dale played his Lute here!
Time stands still.

Helen

A Temple to Water

If the swimming iron fish could speak
what tales they'd tell
of watery dreams
in deep sandstone wells.

Escaped from pools,
ensnared by wrought iron curls
wrapped around columns,
metal tendrils unfurl.

Exotic blooms, birds caught mid flight
bask enraptured in rainbow-glass light.
Metal donkeys nod their silent, gliding beams,
pump and pull, pull and pump in a strict regime.

Living, breathing beasts
puffing steam around
bow to water gods
hidden within the ground.

Anita

Druids Altar

Full of mystery, purpose unknown,
tall and grand, majestic stone.
Hidden away, hard to find,
your eventual arrival clears the mind.
Spiritual healing, a guiding hand,
energy flowing across the land.
Sunrise alignment, a man made hole,
being there feels good for the soul.
Ancestors gathered from far and wide,
connecting together, with sacred pride.
Now neglected and cast aside,
rarely visited, it's power denied.
Modern life with contemporary ways,
transported into a different phase.

Marie

A Young Boy at Papplewick Mill

Sent from London to Papplewick,
a workhouse boy was I.

Working eleven hours a day,
chosen for being a slip of a boy.

Collecting cotton reels we did
They called us boys in Papplewick.

We worked and worked until we dropped,
dusty, smelly, dangerous places.

Deadly coughs of old men and women,
the smell never left me.

Some of me mates died,
Buried in an unmarked grave.
No time to grieve.
No time to be a child.

Helen

Lock Keeper's Cottage

Looking from a window above,
winter sun within a bright blue sky.
Frozen lakes, frozen branches,
frost is here, there and everywhere.
Patches of ice glisten.
A lone man walks by the lock,
his feet crunching in snow, not leaving a trail.
He fastens his coat tightly attempting to keep warm,
slowly turning he heads indoors,
warms his hands by the open fire,
dancing flames and spitting logs transfix his gaze.
He stares out of the window,
and then he's gone!

Helen

Is *Edwin* Here?

Did you travel with me
as I followed your last journey?
Skirting round this forest
to where the path skips quickly
over Mansfield Road, continuing
on the other side.
Were you with me in the dapple and
the dark, hidden away
from lost battles?

Ferns envelope the echoes, shadows
become new allies, each twist of an oak
an open hand to safe passage.
Do we choose the days we waste
as the mist clears, rolls away
too late for this world
in time for the next?
Still there is the need to connect
in prayer, in solace,
in the cool green of a dawn chorus
till the mortar crumbles, the stone migrates.
Now only X marks the spot.

Wendy

Blidworth Churchyard

Bluebells bloom above as we lay
gazing across fields folding distantly away,

sunshine warms our bared bones,
free from flesh, worries unknown.

Forget-me-nots encircle our home
give hope our names engraved in stone

will be recalled by those who trace
their way around this resting place.

In legend Will Scarlet is here concealed,
true or not we will not say

our lips forever sealed.

Anita

Disinvestment

Changed communities
brutally ripped to pieces
never to return.

Lost purpose no pride
their artificial escape
desperate decline.

Marie

Threshold

Observe the countryside
Utopia for free
Tangles of brambles
Dandelions on the breeze
Operatic hedgerows
Orchard boughs sweep
River tumbled pooh sticks
Sunshine warmed feet

Observe down town
Under concrete lights
Tarmac like snakeskin
Datura fuelled fights
Overpass hissing
Ohms on remand
Rivers of obsidian
Street life and damned

Wendy

Knowing Not Seeing

Picture a buttercup,
you think you know.
The colour bright yellow,
your chin aglow.
But look again
and you will see
all you have missed
by imagining me.

Marie

Another Beautiful Day

Staring into space
Seeing nothing
Eyes glazed
Head full
Thoughts racing
Missing out
Another beautiful day
      Gone

Marie

Karma

Why are you like this?
You change like the wind
one minute a friend
the next my enemy.

One day the wind will change
you will be held to account.
What goes around comes around
the tide will turn on you.

Helen

Jog On

I'm not going to stop jogging.
Why should I?
Why should I, to need to feel safe?

A street, the park, a lane,
it shouldn't matter who I meet.

I'm not going to stop jogging.
Why should I?
Why should I, to need to feel safe?

If you're not safe to be out there,
stay home, stay away.

I'm not going to stop jogging.
Why should I?
Why should I, to need to feel safe?

Learn to respect yourself,
your mother, your sister and me.

I'm not going to stop jogging.
Why should I?
Why should I, to need to feel safe?

If you know you can't be trusted,
stay home, stay away.

I'm going to keep jogging.
You are going to stay away.

Marie

Earthbound

I hear sounds of life moving
beneath your skin.
Time ticking,
ageing, fading us.
I lay bound by thoughts and fears.
Is the person I first met
still in this body next to me?
Unrecognisable to ourselves,
we've flown to the moon and back,
used up all our fuel. We sit together,
earthbound.
Now and then, then and now,
such distant points.
My mother's kitchen where we first kissed
belongs to someone else now,
like your love for me.

Anita

It's on the Table

Waiting in the kitchen
part of the family
always here.
Ever deepening furrows
anchor place settings.
Tea rings hint at
small-hour confessions.
Layers of candle wax
nestle deep and dark
along the grain.
Fresh journey lines etch and
map the ordnance
of each new sitting
as memories exchanged
gain credence,
undulate through time,
part of the patchwork.
There's always room
round our old table
you'll be welcomed
like hot chestnuts
on a cold
frosty
day.

Wendy

A Surprise Meeting

Stripy tops, long tops,
blue, yellow and green tops.
A friendly face was smiling.
'Hello Helen', she said.
We chatted and laughed,
about old things and new.
Drinking a coffee or two,
It had been a long time since we met,
At first, I could not remember,
whatever was her name?
Maureen, Pauline, Lotty or Dotty?
Luck would have it, she mentioned Pauline,
so she never knew I had forgot.

Helen

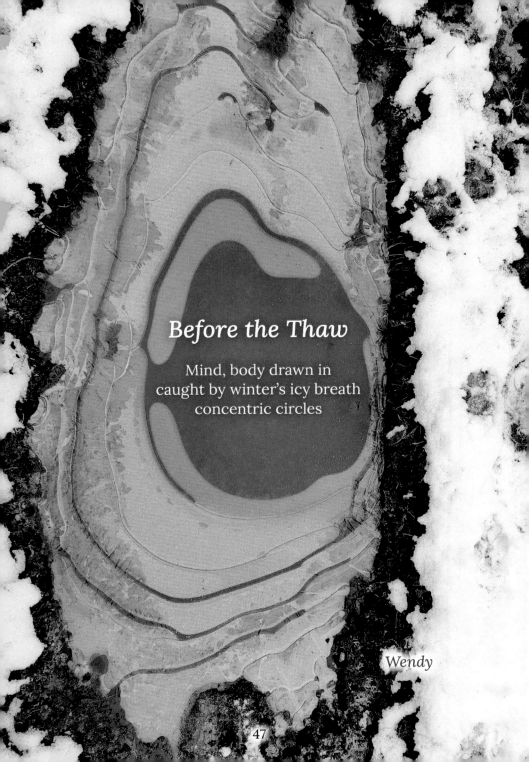

Before the Thaw

Mind, body drawn in
caught by winter's icy breath
concentric circles

Wendy

Christmas Comes Crowding

Shadows in torchlight
snow floating
through still air
winter meeting
the water's edge.
This perfect landscape
just as remembered
something solid
a found charm,
holding your hand,
light as a leaf.
It will get colder
away from the others,
so far away yet,
in the firelight
all of them with me
ever that evening.

Wendy

Winter Wonderland

Looking from a window above,
stillness and calm.
Frozen lakes, frozen branches,
birds singing and skating.
The seasons ever changing,
every moment as precious as before.

Helen

Christmas Spirit

I tried to find the spirit of Christmas,
looked for it everywhere.
It could not be found this year, not even in the air.
I looked for it on the High Street, hoping to find it there,
the only thing that I could see was gloom and despair.

I found the spirit of Christmas at Clipstone Village Hall,
children arrived in good time to play games and have a
ball.
The room decorated with tinsel and holly,
carols in the background, everyone is jolly.
The aroma of food filled the air,
everything smelt good,
turkey, mince pies and even a Christmas pud.
Rumours spread around the hall, Santa was on his way,
then in the distance the sound of bells,
was it Santa's sleigh?

HO, HO, HO in he walked with his great white beard,
children danced around with joy and all the adults
cheered.
Each child was given a present from underneath the tree,
wrapping paper thrown to the floor, faces filled with glee.

Next was time for dancing and singing festive rhymes,
feeling love from all around, precious family time.
Finally, it was over, the party was all done,
time to get home for the special day,
Merry Christmas everyone.

Helen

Epiphany Passing

In the beginning
there was a list
written in black
written in earnest
something to follow.
Two days later
lines appeared
recording in red
recording in earnest
steps had been taken.
Day 4
did not
go well
the list
grew
the paper
groaned
Yet with the new dawn
solution drove motion
persistence in gold
persistence in earnest
Oh! the thrill of achievement.
Mission accomplished
wassail in hand
rejoicing in earnest
rejoicing
in black ink
on a new
blank
page

Wendy

A Gap in Time

All the time in the world

Snap time
Home time
Bedtime

Time flies

Time is of the essence
Time waits for no-one
Living on borrowed time

Time Immemorial

Time heals
Time present, time past
Time will tell

Marie

Facebook Etiquette

I 'liked' your post on Facebook yesterday
but I have to say
my finger clicked before I was aware.
I tried to take back my like,
but it only changed to 'I care'.

I prodded and poked the screen,
moving through emotions
from hysterical laughter to floods of tears.
Whatever I did, it would not disappear.

I gave up, moved on, thought no-one will see,
but now a message has appeared
asking if I'd like to follow you
and that you want to follow me.

Anita

53

Friends for Lunch

On a bed of
ruby lollo rosso and
iron clad spinach
barley twists of bacon recline.
Torques of red onion
sweet orange pepper wheels
recumbent cucumber curls
relax, entwined.
Cheery cherry tomatoes
- seeds exposed,
daintily shield their modesty
with lacy discs of radish,
watch, as spears of spring onion
cast off their jackets,
surf on herby waves of oil
glide purposefully into
parcels of chicken
so they

tumble
slowly,
gathering whispers
of fennel
walnut shavings,
pepper bombs
primed to explode
then gently
from above
fluttering frayed flakes
of parmesan
drift,
alight,
gain purchase.
The salad submits,
we raise our forks.

Wendy

Food of Love

Your kisses were inside the rhubarb crumbles,
warmth of a hug hidden in stews
with their fluffy dumplings of love.
Blackberries, purple pieces of your heart,
preserved in jams and pies.
Our summertime caught,
saved
for approaching winter days
when you were no longer here.

Anita

Come in, sit down

curious coat hooks stand
to attention
display their
rusty medals
expectant chairs nurse
cushions, keep
threadbare
arms hidden
lotions, potions, dried
up remnants still fail to
reclaim what was lost
knick knacks knocked over
last Christmas
gaze enviously
as silken webs
spiral above them
on the breeze
reconnecting
a mother and son
faces fading with the light

Wendy

Will There Be Room?

Lovingly decorated, in neutral hues,
gifts piled high,
not yet used.
The world is ready for you to arrive,
yet there's a niggle,
deep inside.

I know what to do, I know what to say
but how will my heart feel when
you arrive,
today.

Will there be space,
will there be room,
will the magic of love consume?

Marie

Incomer

I arrived from a small northern place
near the coast
to the centre of England
far from the sea.
I planned to stay for a year,
to study and expand my wings.
They took me under their wing
and introduced me to their treasures,
the highs and lows
of Goose Fair and the City Ground.

Theirs became mine
and mine became hers,
passed to the next generation.
It became her home, her treasure,
our hearts full of love.

Marie

The Sound of Trees

Plug a USB into a tree,
listen to their stirrings.

Winds swirl around
tickling
tips of poplars until
they erupt into giggles.

Chestnut trees click
making spiky green cases
wrapped tightly around
glossy brown conkers.

Sycamores with their whirligigs,
whizz and hum,
spin towards the ground,
keys to open the world.

Magnolia quietly budding
explode
with a bang
into china teacup blossoms.

A king oak
majestically stands
contemplating centuries.
Silently.

Anita

Marked by Stones

Emerald, sapphire, garnet
mystical symbols of birth.
Precious crystals hidden within the earth.
Silky smooth pebbles pocketed,
memories of a moment captured.

Hard, cold. Carried
within a mother's heart
for a daughter's life,
taken by another's hand.
Bessie's name engraved forever
in flesh and stone.

A final resting place,
carved in granite
millenia in creation.
It whispers 'look
at all I have survived'.
She shares its immortality.

Anita

New Age Traveller

Every journey has its need
of optimism, wise preparation
yet with endless time to ruminate
too much experience becomes
her over full backpack,
guarding old adventures
protecting how life was,
something to fall back on?
In this 'needs met' room
hard wearing carpet draws a path
to an open door.
From her straight backed chair
with seatbelt firmly fastened
forever facing forward
she lets another dream unfold.
Her last adventure.

Wendy

Parley with a Badger

Settled within a spreading oak
Badger raised his noble head,
a creaking cart fell silent,
the Keeper of the Forest paused,
- he heard her   morning   blessing.
Twice, hunting royals stopped by,
convening to save the realm
disguised by shadows and ivy,
speaking quietly, in privacy,
- he heard every   whispered   word.
Lost boundaries had Dukes worrying,
as the navy increased demand,
busy tenants went whistling by
axemen rocked the ground
- he heard fellow   patriarchs   crashing.
After double-decker Roughnecks
foraged oil beneath his roots, their
long worn tracks became highways;
21st century Foresters commute
- he heard children   gather   acorns.
Eight hundred years spent listening
part of the Parliament Oak,
destined to watch and wait
willing to share Sherwood's legends
- he hears phoenix   rise   again.

Wendy

614 Bells

Up and down we go, but not without first
stopping, every May, the loud bells calling.
There, a wood of blue, irresistible,
our brief fling with mindful meanderings.
There, for us to see, their calming beauty,
our brief escape from raw ruminations.
Photos taken, memories now restored,
driving blithely down the A614.

Marie

Corvid

You came covid. We didn't invite you
but you came anyway.
Corvid.
A black crow over our lives.
You took our world
and shrank it.

A witches spell covid. A charm covid,
to banish you away.
We repeat your name covid,
take your power away,
to hide you away covid, to make you
go away covid - forever, covid.

We will chant together to evaporate you,
make you rue the day
you even looked our way covid.
Send you back to whence you came covid.
Corvidly you can fly away

covid be gone,
we say, be gone covid.

It's over they say, but still you stay covid.
An unwanted guest at our party, covid,
not knowing it's past your time to leave.
We throw you out covid
with leftover pizza crusts and cold
garlic bread, covid. You belong in the bin,
with your deaths, suffocating breaths.

Unwelcome covid,
unwanted covid,
unrelenting covid.
You are Corvid,
dining out on cadavers.
Black wings
wrapped around our lives.

Be gone covid, we say,
covid be gone.

Anita

My Body is Me

How lucky am I, to have a body like you,
the amazing things you allow me to do.

Beating and breathing, amid the buzzing of bees,
swaying and sweeping, dancing among trees.
Flowing and flailing, running up hills,
smiling and stretching, tasting the thrills.
Skipping and swimming, climbing up fells,
beautiful sights, wonderful smells.

Changing, evolving, for all to see.
I am my body,
my body is me.

Marie

竹

Strong, exotic yet beige.
Feared in war as brutal, yet
the only diet of black and white bears.
Invasive, colonising.
A gift and a pest,
loved and hated.
A prop for peas and beans.
A bowl for rice and noodles.
Found in a park on a summer's day.

Marie

Missing

Happily I gave my time to you,
we sat together for hours.
Contented at first,
gazed lovingly at your beauty,
slowly building our relationship
piece by piece,
creating a picture of our future.
Blue sea, white sand, a boat
anchored in the harbour
poised to escape to distant lands.
But towards the end it became clear,
from your thousand promises
something was missing.
Feeling incomplete, I left you Jigsaw.

Anita

Cat-atonic

Slinkily I may emerge from my hidden spot
where I have lain for hours
watching you call my name,
begging for my return.

I am here, undisclosed,
content and comfortable
stomach full of illicit kill
no need to move or let you know
I am safe and well.

You are nothing to me
until
I am hungry again.

Anita

You Left a Shirt

The door creaks open
you're waiting, buttons
and collar askew,
arms seam-defined.
Peering beyond,
over your shoulder
into the half light,
see others hanging round,
subtle shades of
possible lives to come
but they can't share
what you shared.
Sun warmed rocks
sting of salty air
salad cream and sand,
a terminal announcement.
Absence doesn't have
to mean without,
there's always a
choice, you told us.
Sliding my arms into yours
try to breathe you in
I roll up your sleeves and
together, we oil the door.

Wendy

74

Uhtceare (Ucht-kay-ara)

When thoughts take over from sleep,
before birds sing,
before dawn chases darkness away.
When hearts are more aware of loss,
of youth, of friends, of love.
Invisible future envisioned,
problems crowd.
I yearn to change the past, predict my future.
Be fearless moving through
this compilation of life.
I want to reach out
hold you close, feel your heart rhythm,
calm my beats to match yours,
breathe in your sleep,
capture it to make it mine.
But I lay still,
unwilling to break your dreams.

Anita

Knock Knock

tilt the blind
turn off the lamp
watch duvet clouds
settling over the
dark, empty road
encircling the lights
that reveal raindrops
submitting to the wind
turn off Heartbeat
outside comes closer
behind the horizontals
branches squawk,
scour the glass
boxed rosemary taps
repeats her appeal
window frame creaks
cherry tree leaks
penultimate leaves
twisting shadows
bow and curtsey
fall in line, skip apart
here and gone with
the rhythm of a
winter caller

Wendy

Her Spirit

Anna feels lonely, remembers better times,
she climbs steep stairs, wishing for warmth.
November has turned everything cold,
icicles hang inside windows.
After much debate, she picks a jumper,
blue is her favourite colour.
She watches logs on a fire and instantly feels calm,
distracted by orange dancing flames.
A thundering sound,
a coal train speeds by.
The house shakes and rattles,
three more carriages than yesterday.
Blue is still her favourite colour.

Helen

Make Room

Give a body room
to breathe,
to grow,
to explore
what is unknown,
for now.
To dream,
to take first steps
along new paths
untrod by those before.
To blaze a trail,
to be unique,
to become
yourself.

Anita

Tailor Made

It's time for bed
the lights go out
last waking thoughts
escape as a sigh
meander into
another room where
they're suspended
over his bench.

Checking the time
he sits down, begins,
pulls common threads
binds areas of concern
looks for the relevant
re-shapes sorrows
drawing in hope
drawing in starlight.

Your tapestry grows
cascades and ripples
across the floor to
wrap you in dreams.

Wendy

Who Knew

Who knew
if you stop,
sit quiet
and close your eyes,
a whole new world,
opens up,
both inside
and out.

A heartbeat,
a breath,
an ease
of tension.
A church bell,
a barking dog,
a hum
of distant traffic.

From above,
she already knew,
the way of things,
the way of the world.
She knew
they were there,
waiting
for you to notice.

Marie

Notes

Cover image
Reproduced with the kind permission of Alexandra Ghimisi
from her original painting 'The Path'. A Romanian-born
artist, embarked on her artistic journey in 2016 when she
relocated to the UK to pursue her passion for art. Currently
based in Nottinghamshire, she holds a BA degree, a
testament to her dedication to honing her craft. Alexandra
plays a pivotal role as a part-time Art Tutor with Inspire
Culture, where she imparts painting techniques to adult
learners. As an exhibiting member of the Nottingham
Society of Artists, Alexandra actively contributes to the
local art scene. Through her art, Alexandra invites others to
join her on a visual journey, where dedication and passion,
coupled with her academic achievements, converge to
create a vibrant tapestry of inspiration and creativity.

All Weathers
Photograph courtesy of Marie Armstrong-Keane,
copyright ©2024

A Temple to Water
Image courtesy of Martine Hamilton-Knight,
Papplewick Pumping Station Trust.

Papplewick Pumping Station is a Scheduled Ancient
Monument a little distance outside Ravenshead where
it has stood since the 1880s. It was built to provide clean
water for the residents of Nottinghamshire by Thomas
Hawksley, an eminent water engineer. Born in Arnold,
Nottinghamshire he was responsible for over a hundred
schemes to supply uncontaminated water to families

throughout the county. The pumping station remains in working order and is open to visitors with regular steaming days.

Before the Thaw
Photograph courtesy of David Jackson, copyright ©2024

Blidworth Brass
Photograph courtesy of Marie Armstrong-Keane, copyright ©2024 with kind permission given by Karen Cretney, Blidworth Welfare Band.

Blidworth Churchyard
Photograph courtesy of David Jackson, copyright ©2024

Bread or Blood
The first Luddite disturbance in the country took place in Arnold in 1811 when a group of framework knitters smashed 63 'wide' frames which needed less skill to operate and produced cheaper, inferior quality cloth. Framework Knitters were desperately poor and concerned at the deskilling of their trade by this new equipment, took direct action. Owd Enoch was the nickname of the large lump hammers the Luddites used to smash the iron frames and render them unusable. Frame breaking was made a capital offence in 1812 - with either hanging or transportation the punishment. Lord Byron gave his maiden speech in the House of Commons defending the framework knitters during the debate of the act. In spite of offering significant rewards for information, no Luddite was betrayed by their comrades. John Booth was a Luddite in the Spen Valley in Yorkshire who was injured during an attack on a mill. He and others were interrogated but gave no names. Asking to speak to Reverend Hammond Roberson, his dying words were - 'can you keep a secret? Aye lad, so can I'.

Change
Photograph courtesy of Anita Jackson, copyright ©2024

Clippo
Photograph courtesy of Wendy Riley, copyright ©2024

Druid's Altar
Photograph courtesy of Marie Armstrong-Keane, copyright ©2024

Is Edwin Here?
Photograph courtesy of Wendy Riley, copyright ©2024

Legend has it that Edwin, the first Christian king of Northumbria, was killed in battle near Cuckney in 632 AD. A chapel was built dedicated to him just outside Edwinstowe, St Edwin's Chapel Cross marks its location, erected by the Duke of Portland.

Knowing Not Seeing
Photograph courtesy of Marie Armstrong-Keane, copyright ©2024. The photograph shows a Celandine flower, part of the buttercup family.

Marked by Stones
Bessie Sheppard was just 17 when, walking home from Mansfield to Papplewick on 7 July 1817 after a day seeking work, she was murdered by Charles Rotherham who, finding no money on her, stole her boots and umbrella. He was caught in Loughborough and hanged in Nottingham for his crime. Bessie is buried in Papplewick churchyard and a monument stone funded by public subscription was placed by the side of the A60 by Harlow Wood is still there today.

Papplewick Church
Photograph courtesy of Helen Clarke, copyright ©2024

Parley with a Badger
Photograph courtesy of Wendy Riley, copyright ©2024

Skylark
In response to 'A Green Cornfield' by Christina Rossetti
describing how she paused in a cornfield to listen to a
skylark above her. Christina continued her journey but
knew the bird's song would go on long after she had left.

The Robin
Photograph by A Perry on Unsplash.com, a free to use
image.

The Sound of Trees
Photograph courtesy of David Jackson, copyright ©2024

Uhtceare (ucht-kay-ara)
That moment when you suddenly awake before its light and
your mind is racing over the past, the future, problems -
real or imagined, and sleep eludes. Anglo-Saxons called this
Uhtceare - 'Anxiety before dawn'.

Wellow Dancer
Photograph courtesy of Marie Armstrong-Keane,
copyright ©2024

What Feet
Photograph courtesy of David Jackson, copyright ©2024

614 Bells
Photograph courtesy of Marie Armstrong-Keane,
copyright ©2024